Progressive Patterns Intricate Inspirations Adult Colouring Book

nikk nakk

designs

Progressive Patterns Intricate Inspirations - Adult Colouring Book

Copyright 2015 by nikk nakk designs

Created by Niki Palmer, Ros Tulleners

Illustrated by Stuart Campbell, Subrata Dutta, Elshan Gurbanov,

First edition 2015

ISBN: 978-1-925422-02-3

Don't let the kids have all the fun! Welcome to the pleasure of colouring for adults.

Intricate Inspirations is the third book in the Progressive Patterns series, designed especially for those experienced colourists who are looking for more challenging geometric designs and colouring techniques.

You may like to experiment with the more complex techniques of shading, blending and burnishing to make your masterpieces come alive.

All you really need are some coloured pencils and a good quality pencil sharpener to get started. However, modern art and craft stores are a wonderland - explore the amazing range of pencils, crayons, gel and metallic pens, chalks, watercolour pencils for inspiration.

Just for fun, you may like to start out by trying our 'no fail' pot luck approach!

Make a up of tea or coffee if you need one.
Find a quiet place to work away from electronic distractions.
Let the book fall open at any page.
Close your eyes and pick up any colour.
Choose a shape and start to colour.
There aren't any rules..... just let your imagination run wild.

Soon you will be caught up in your work, your mind will be focused and the realities of the day will drift away. The tension will drain from your body as your pencils reveal the colourful masterpiece under your fingertips..

Try to allocate at least 15 -30 minutes a day to this simple, inexpensive way to calm your mind and body. Most importantly, relax and have fun! The team at nikk nakk designs certainly had fun creating these designs for you to enjoy!

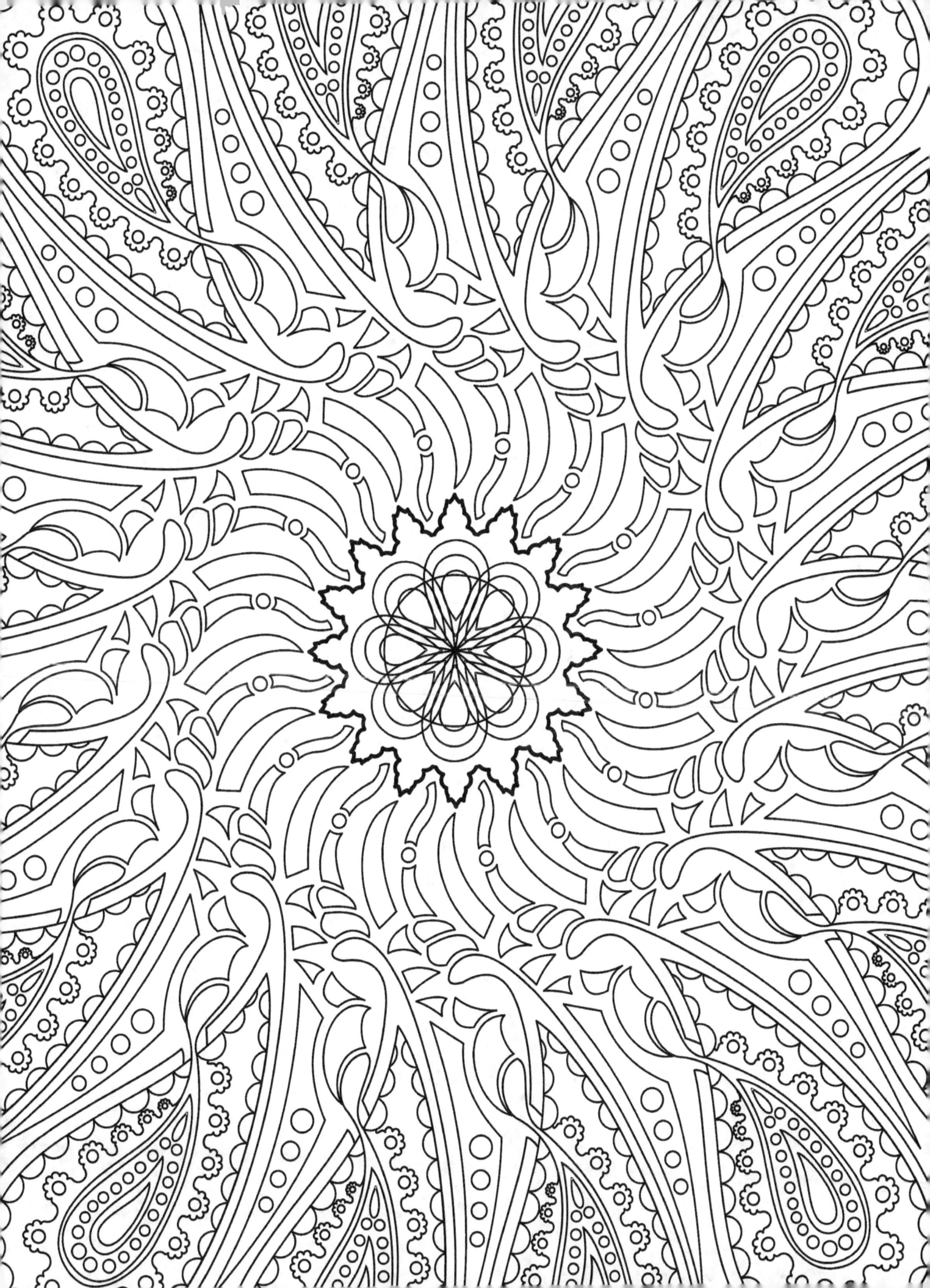

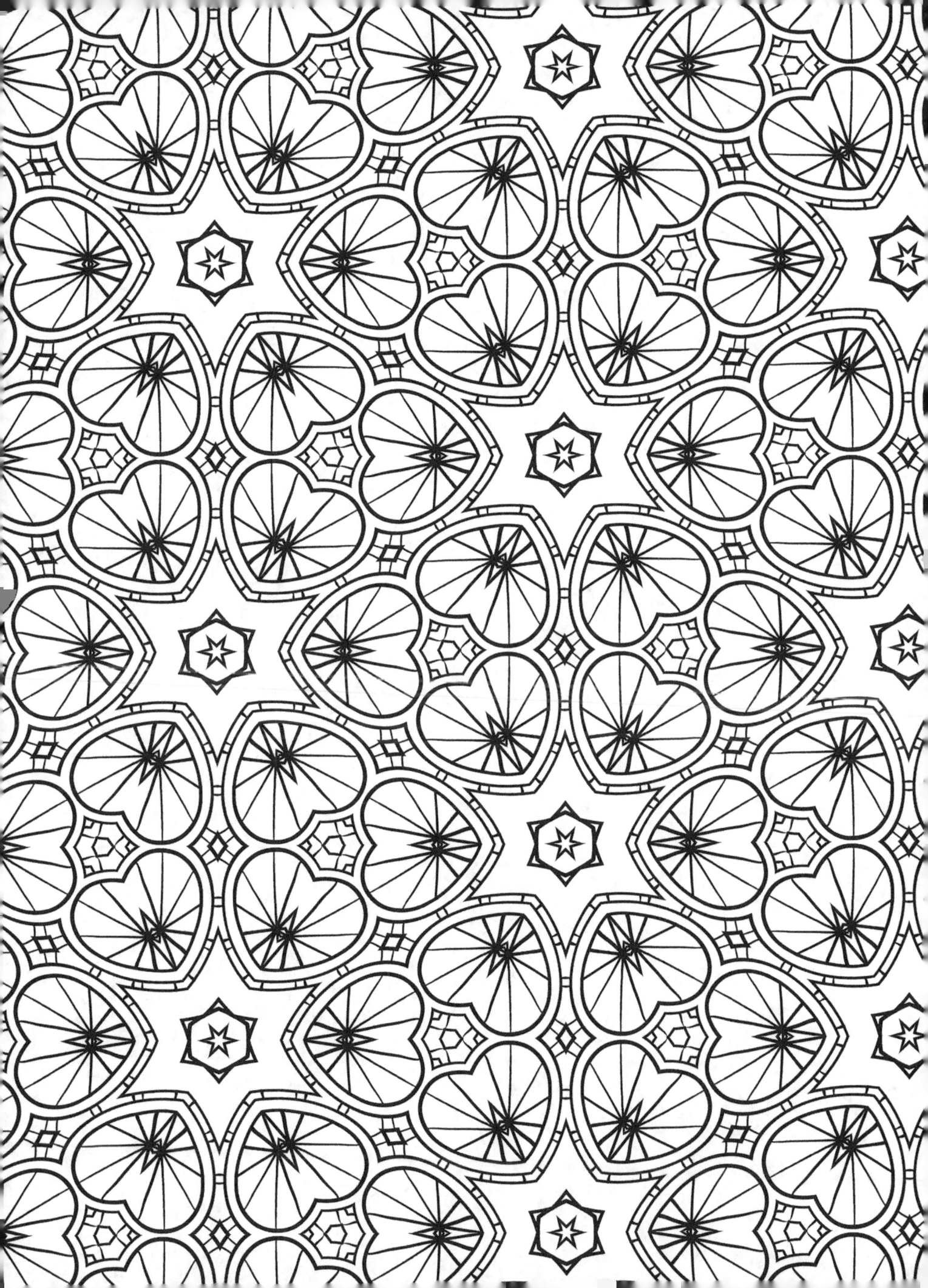

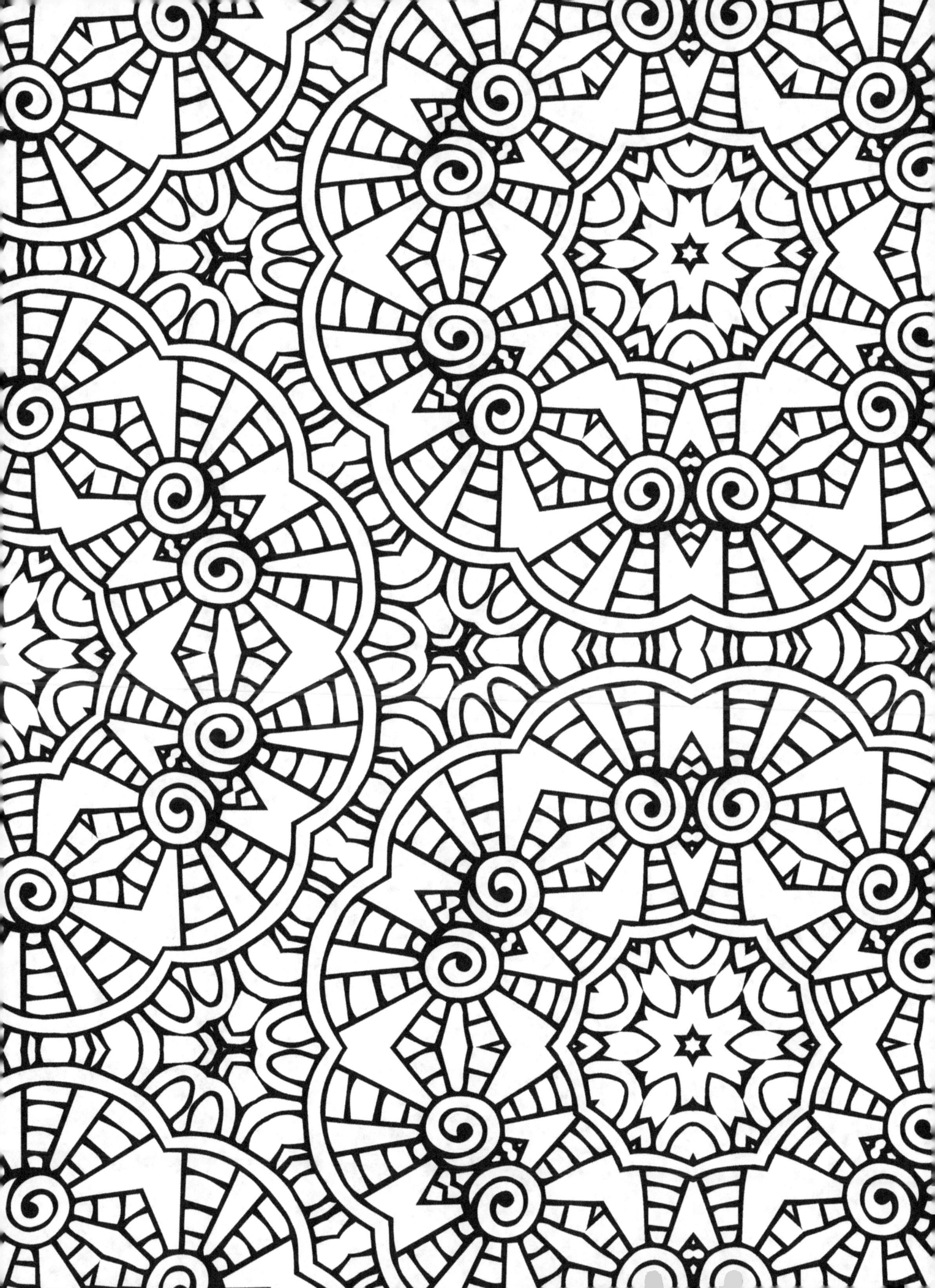

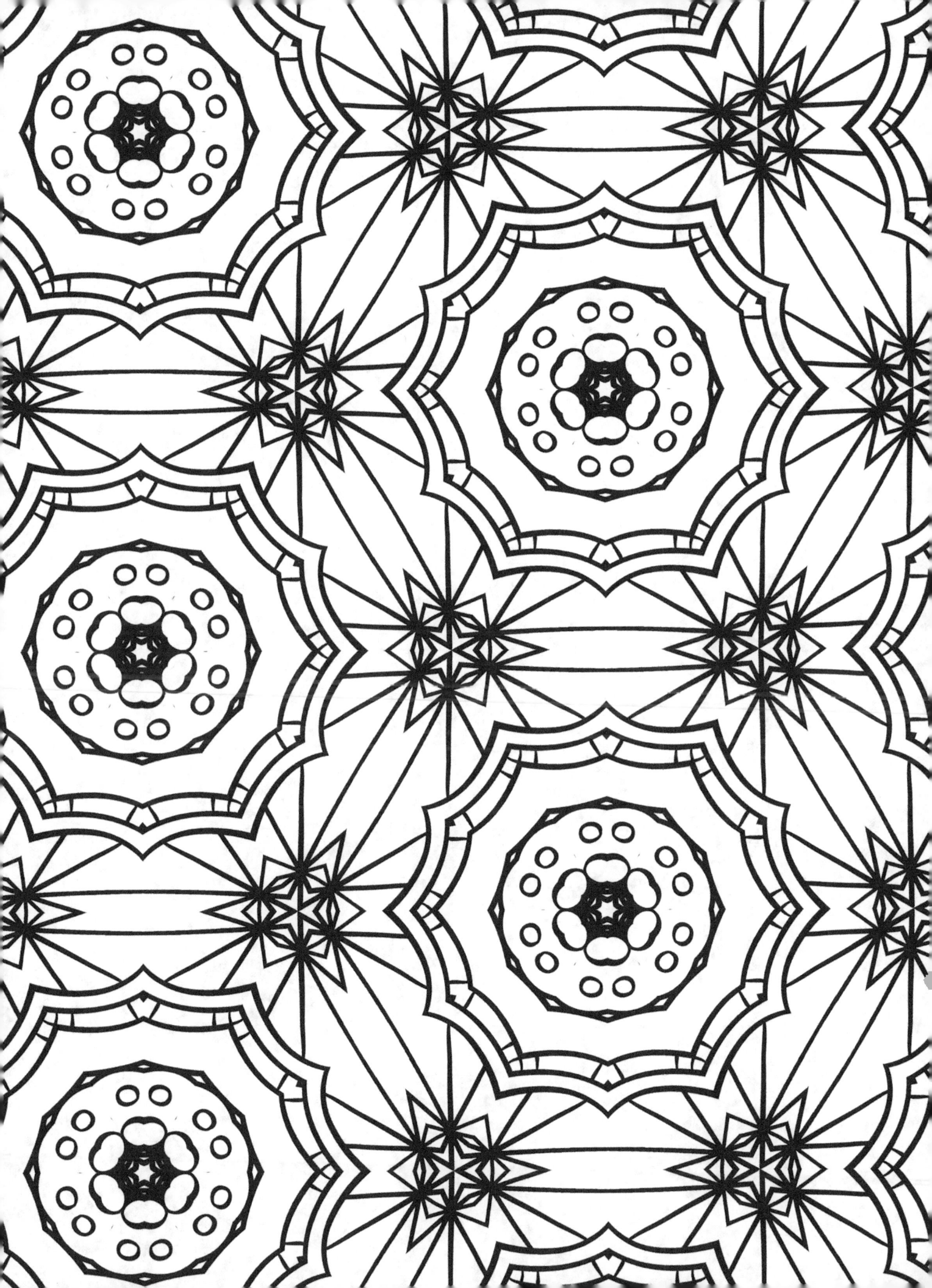

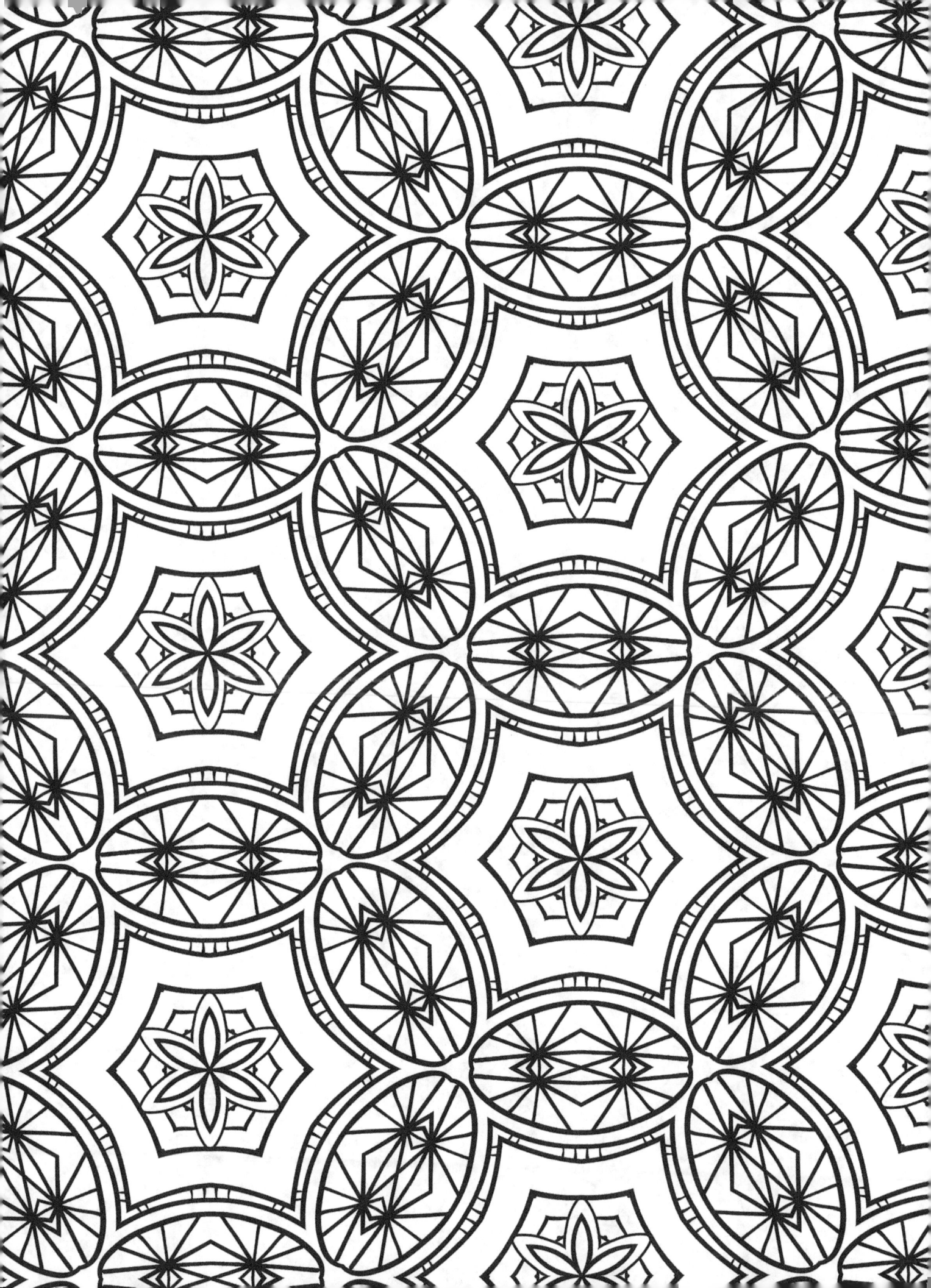

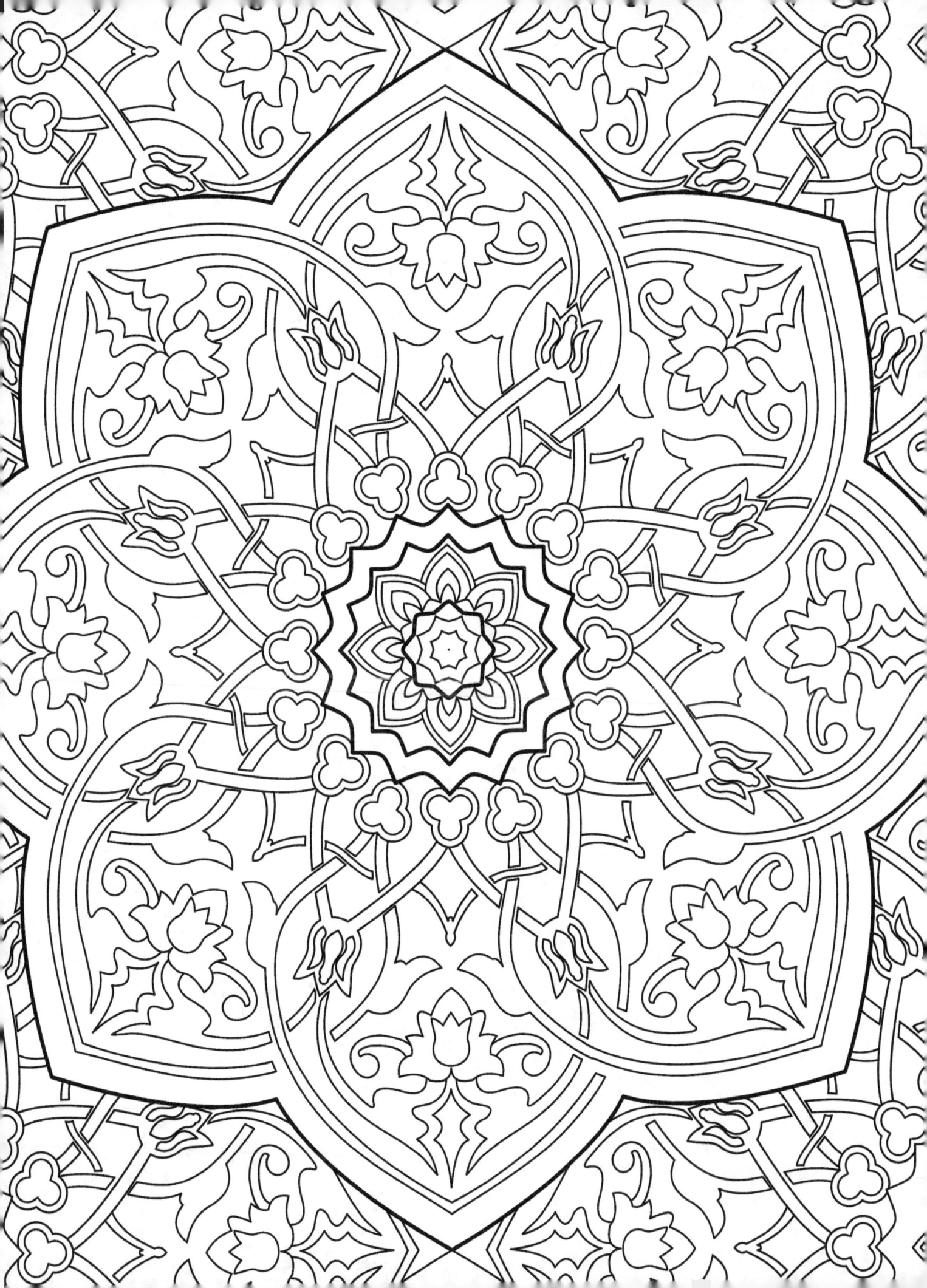

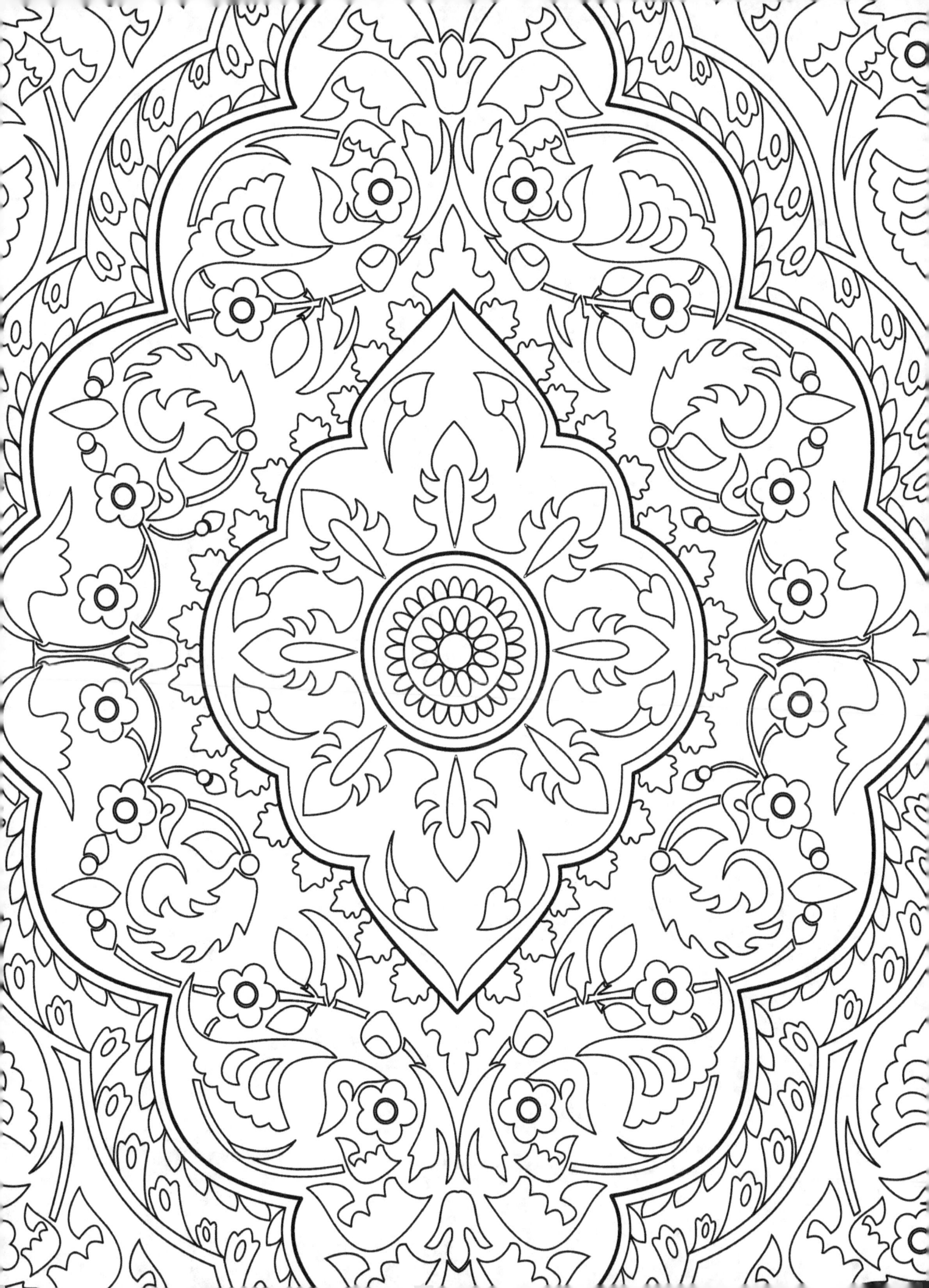

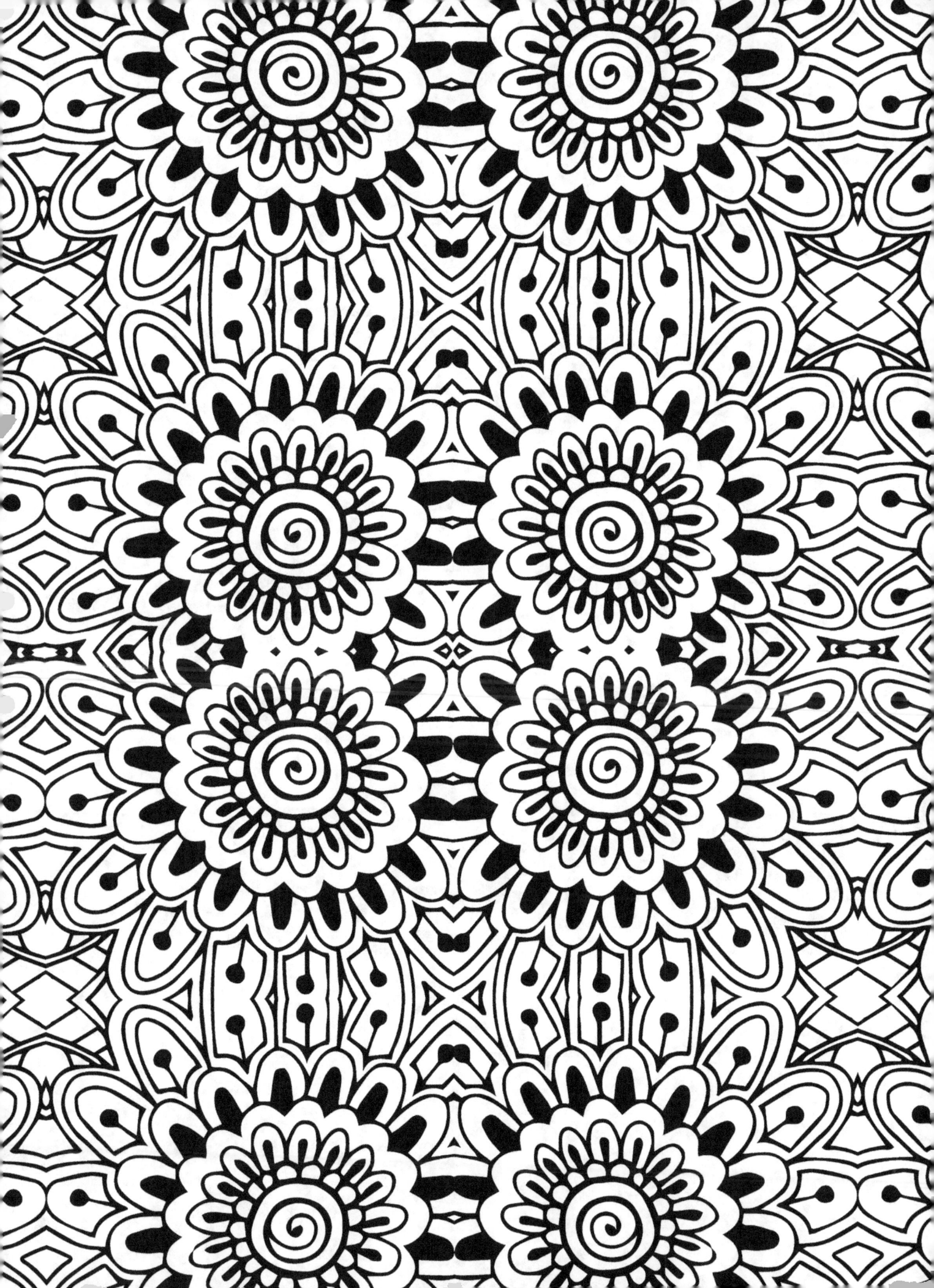

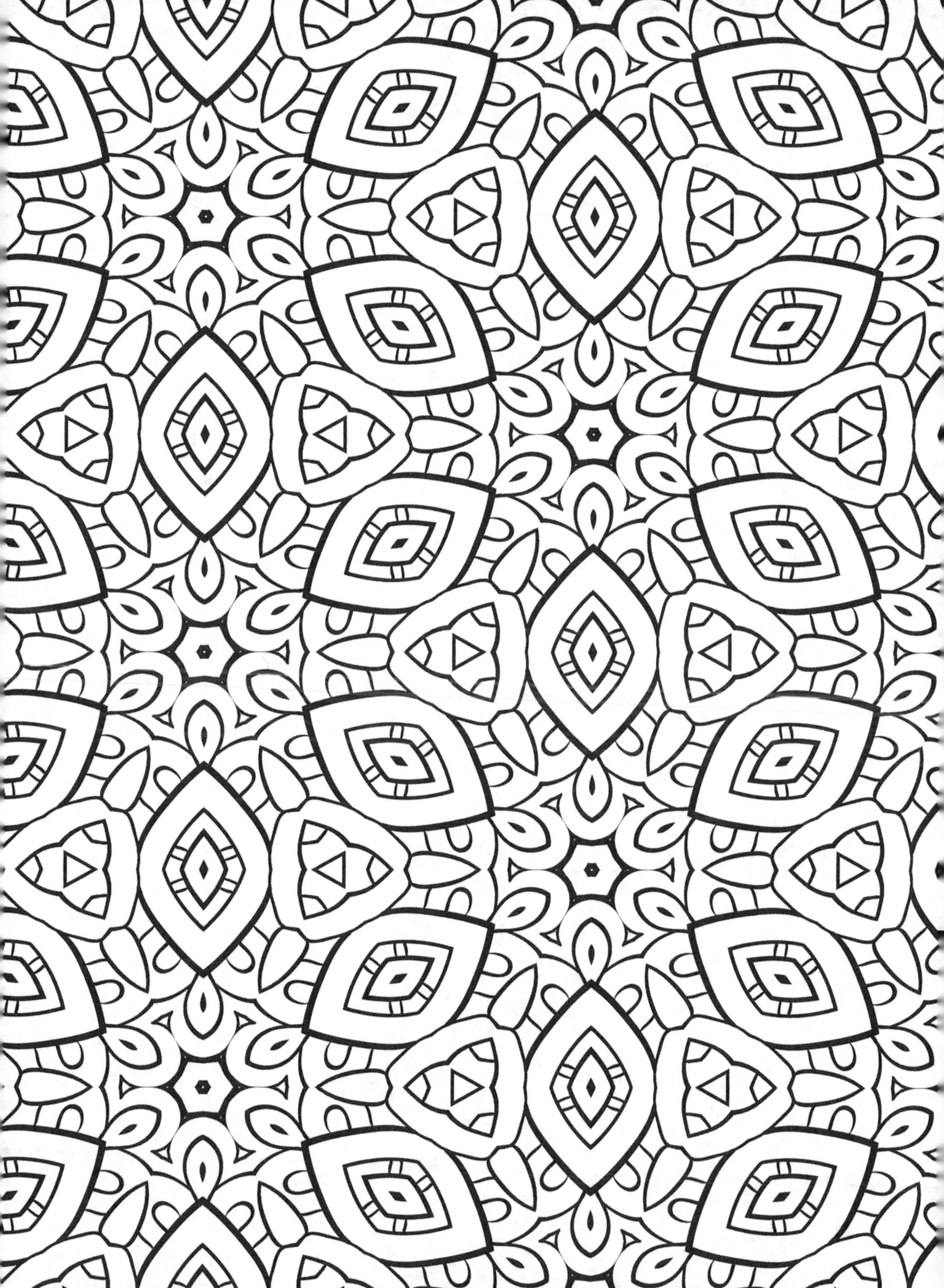

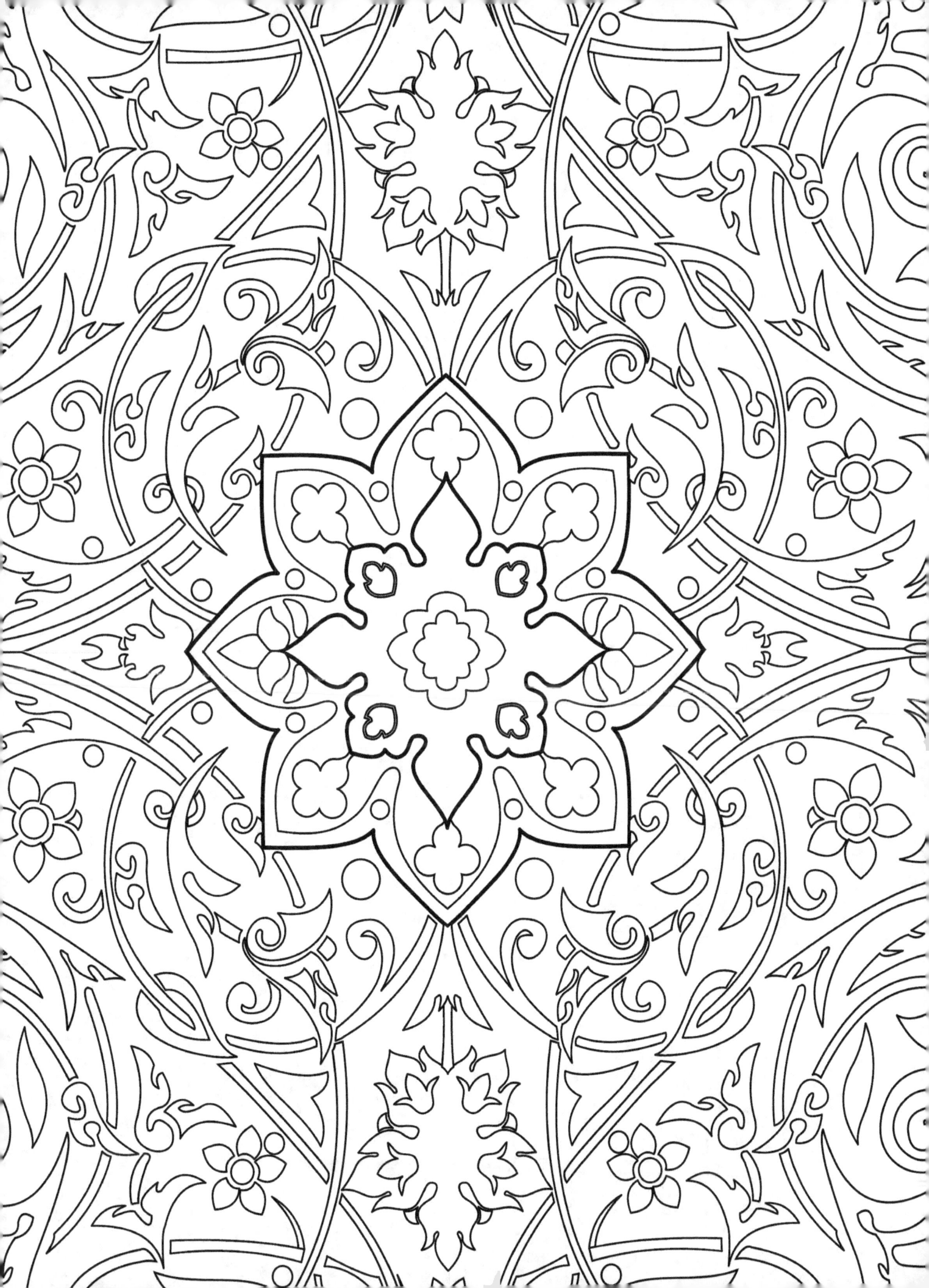

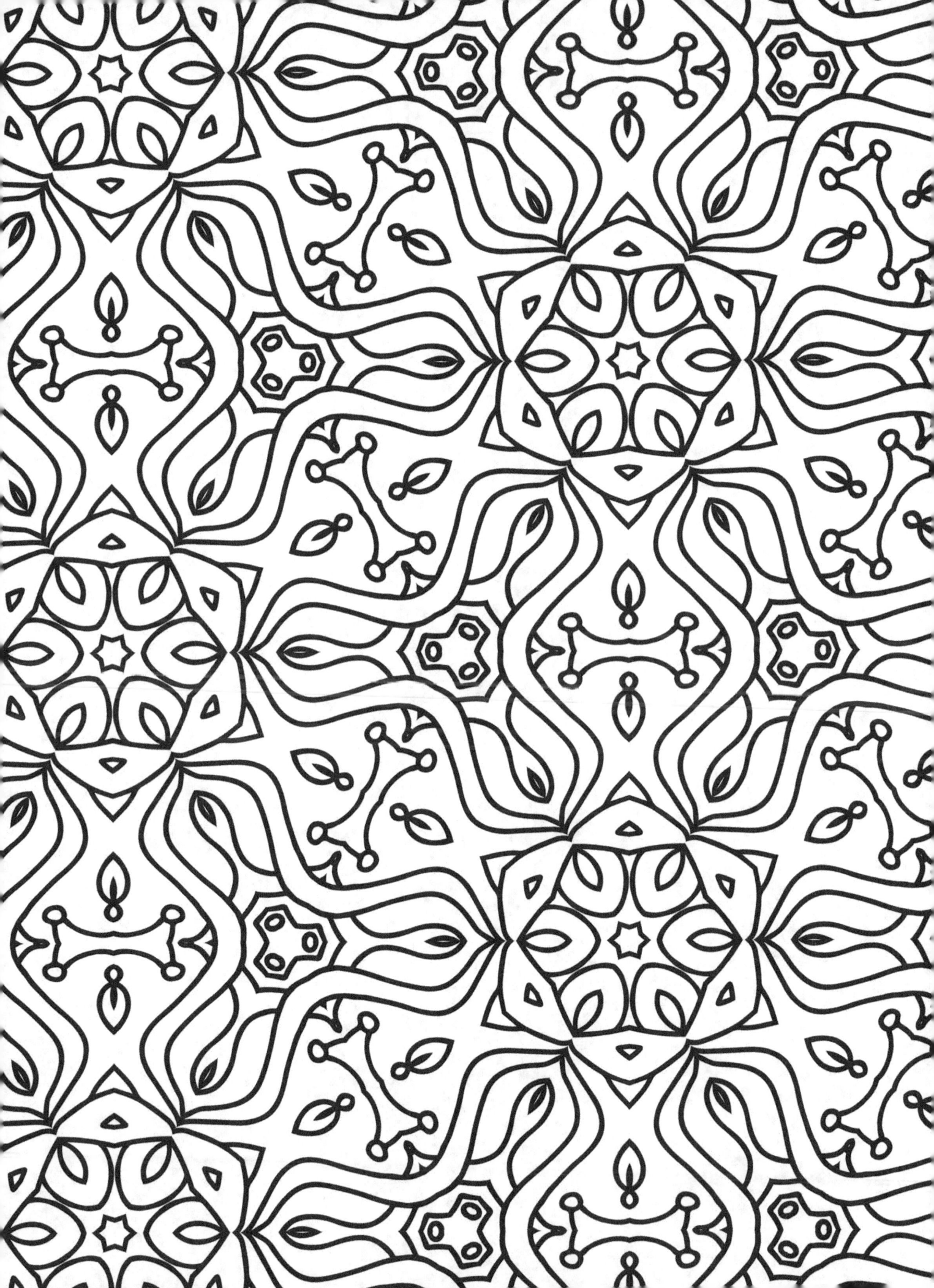

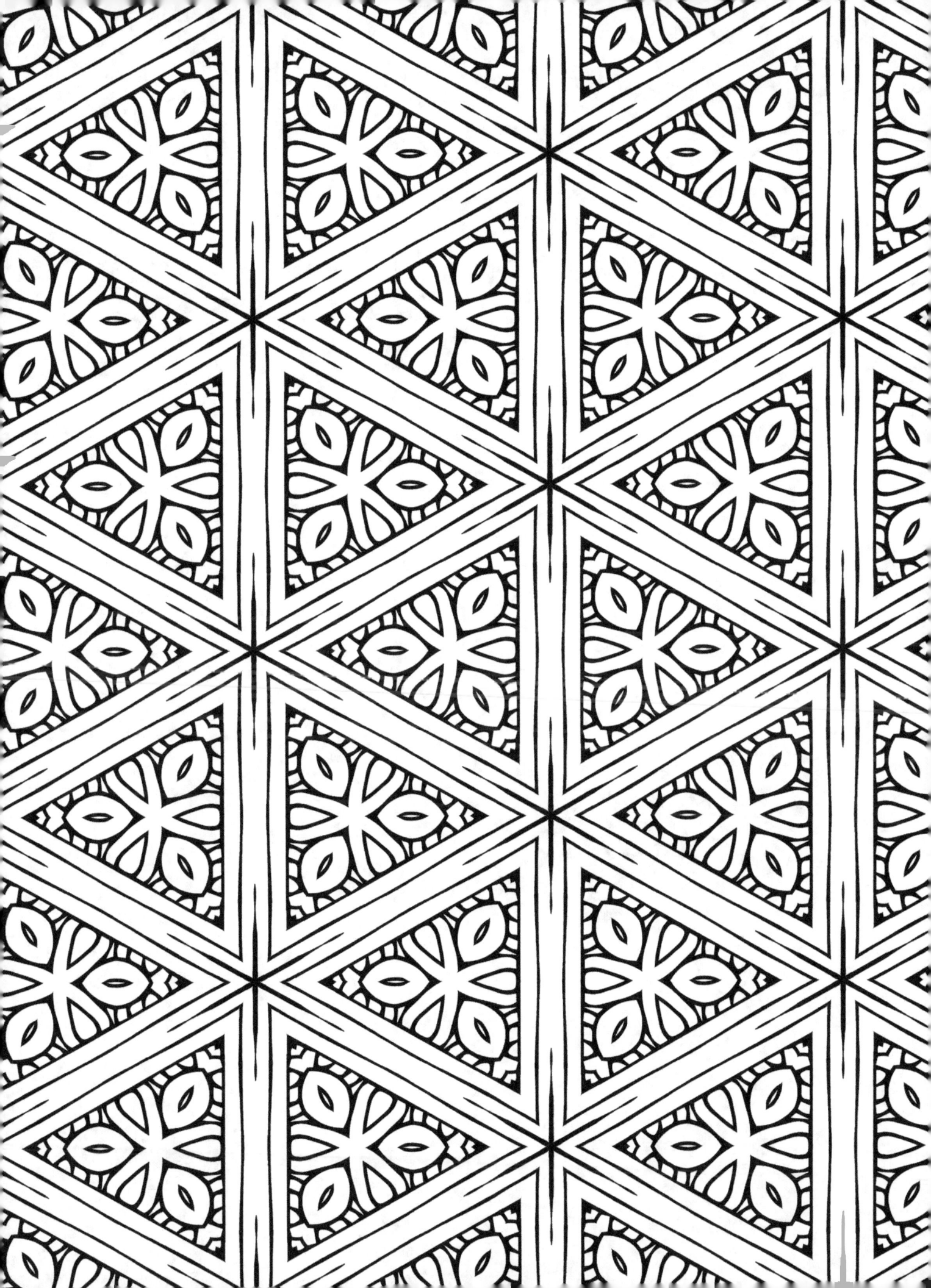

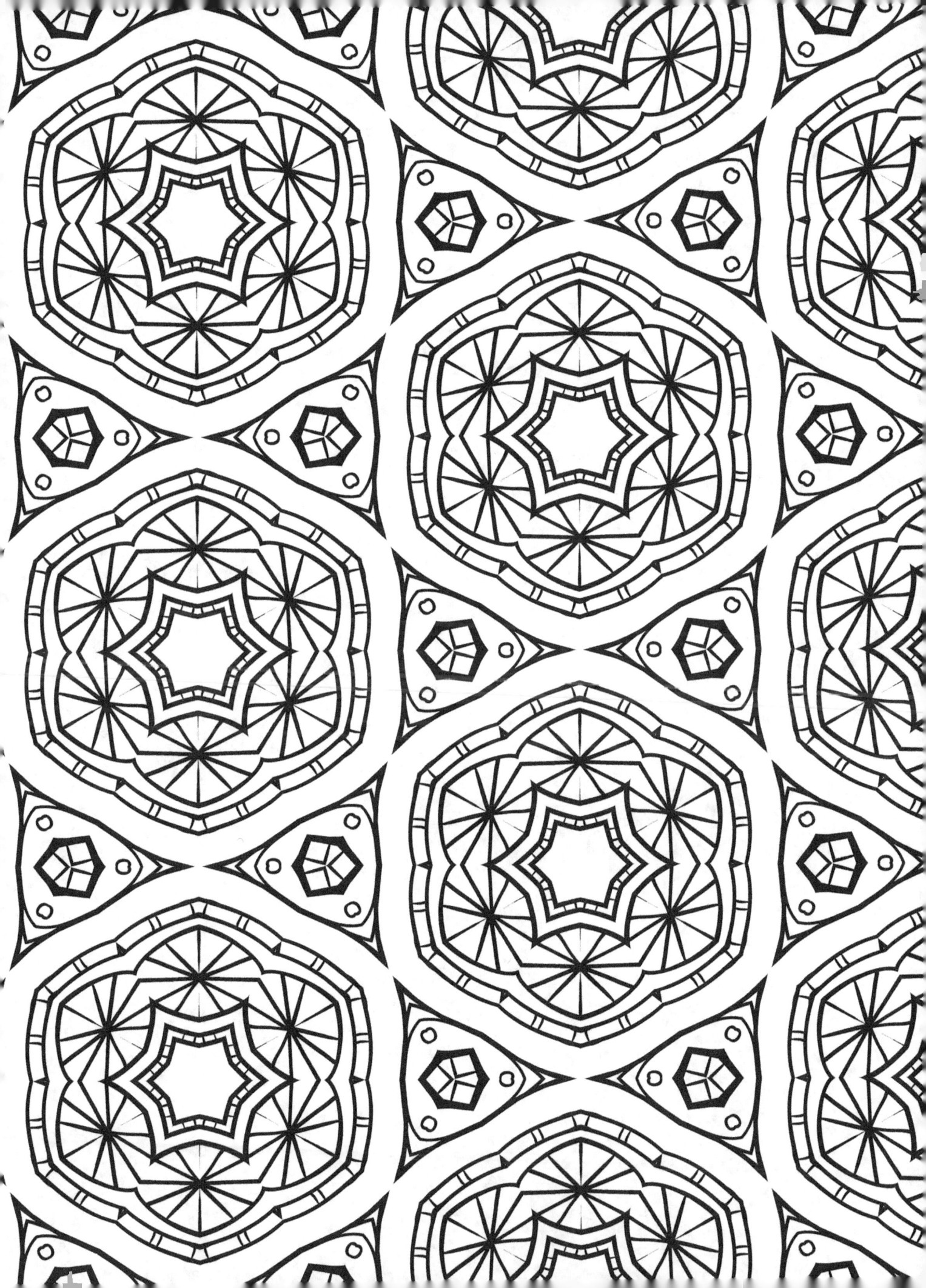

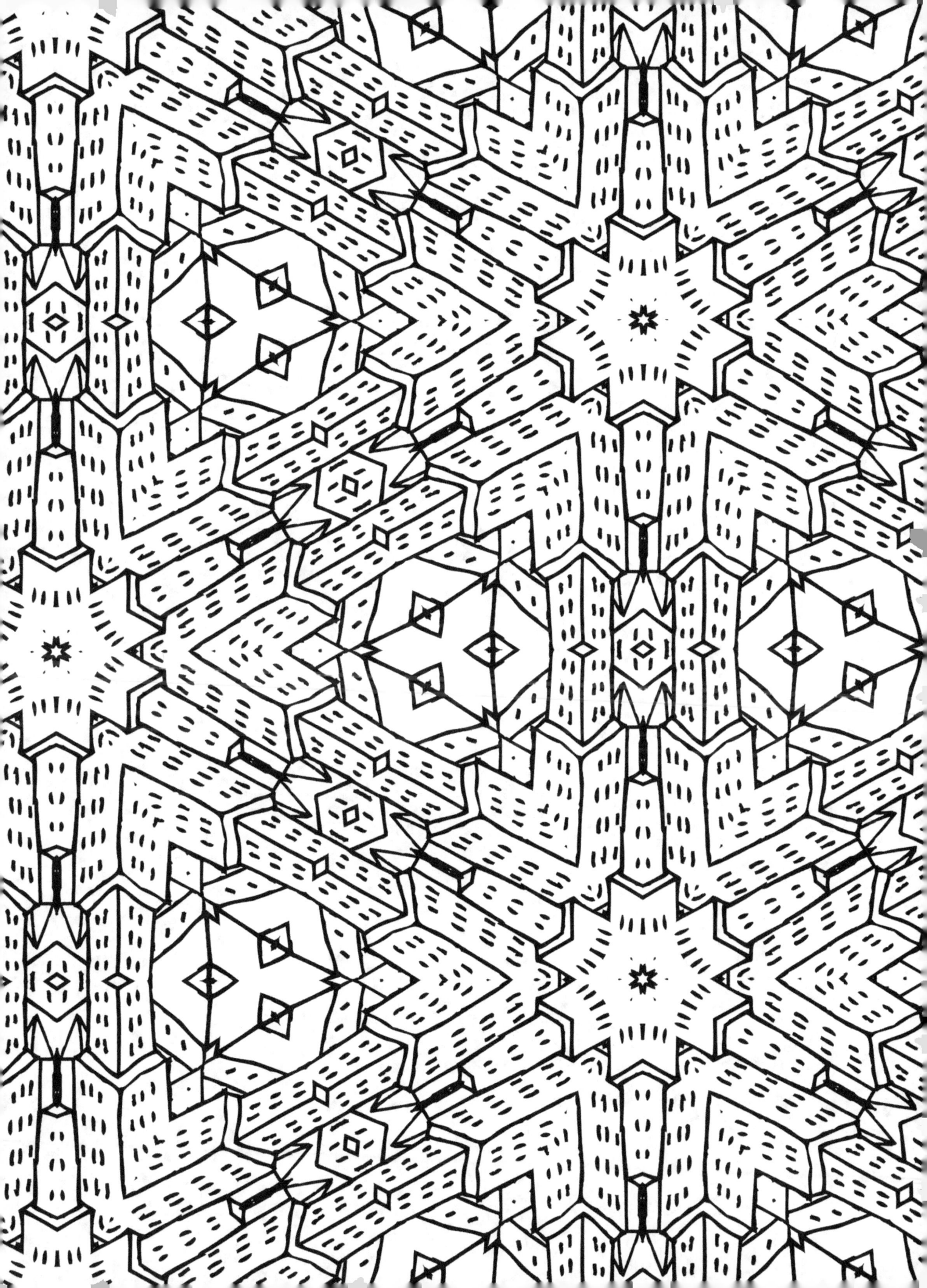

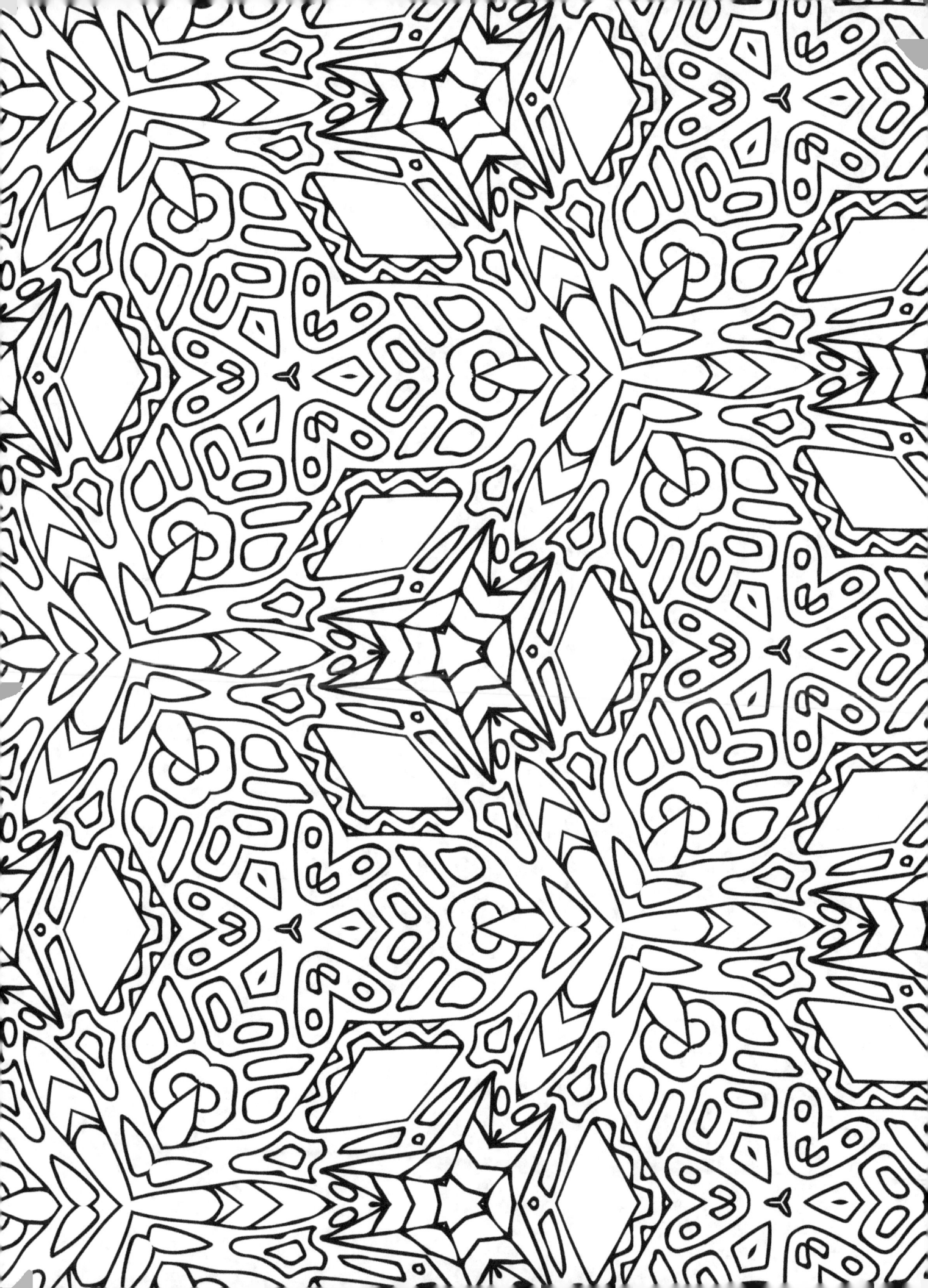

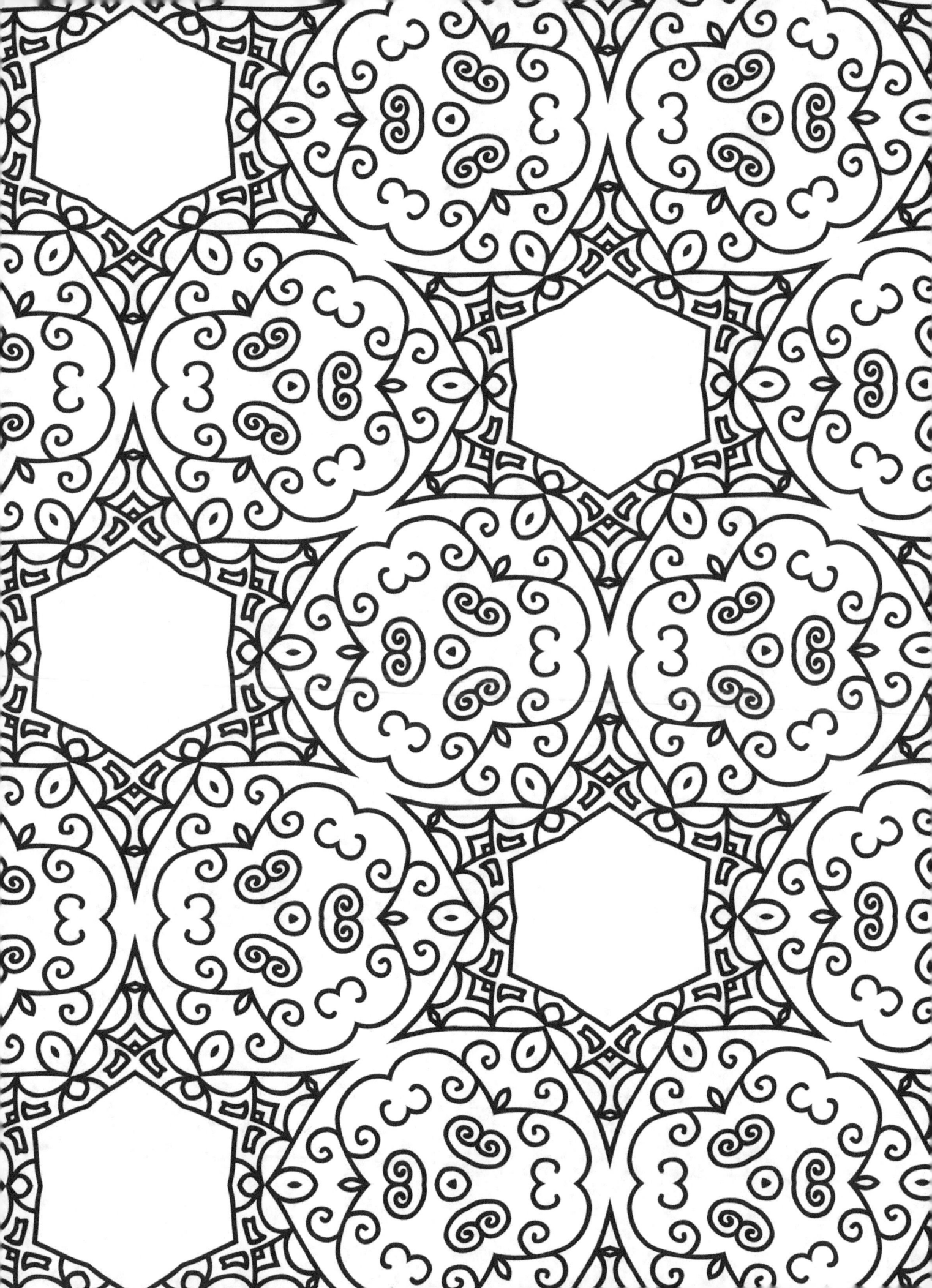

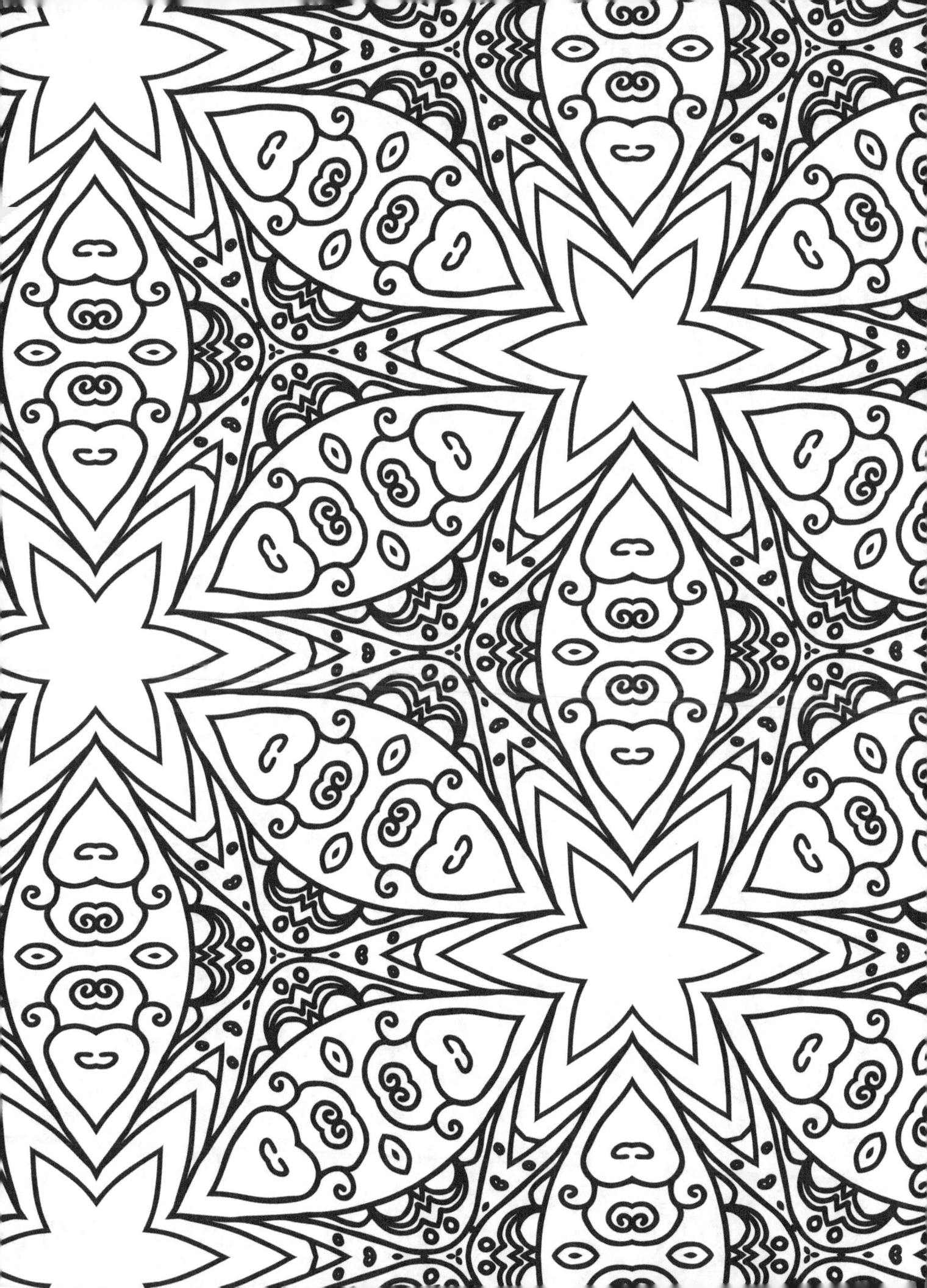

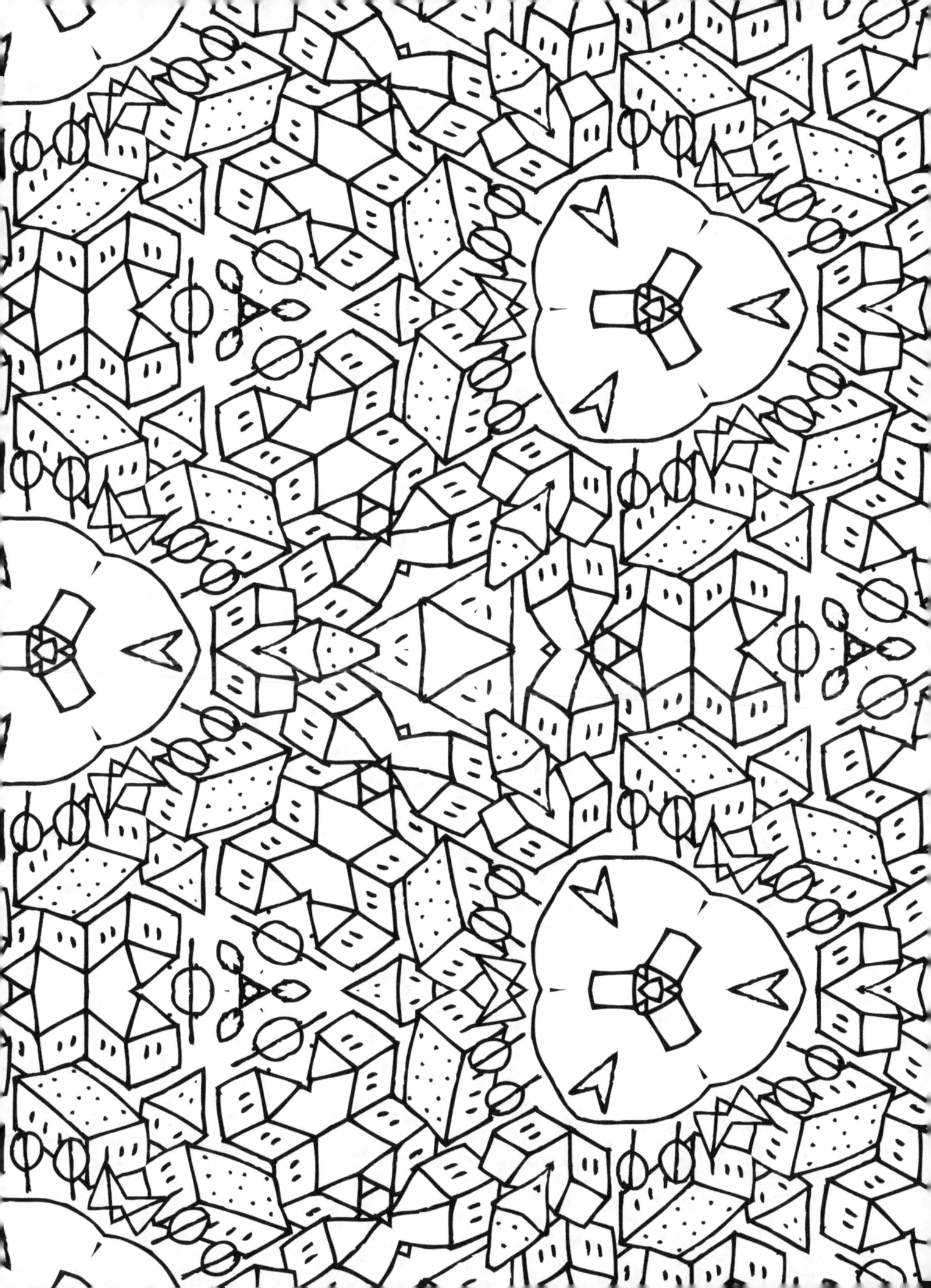

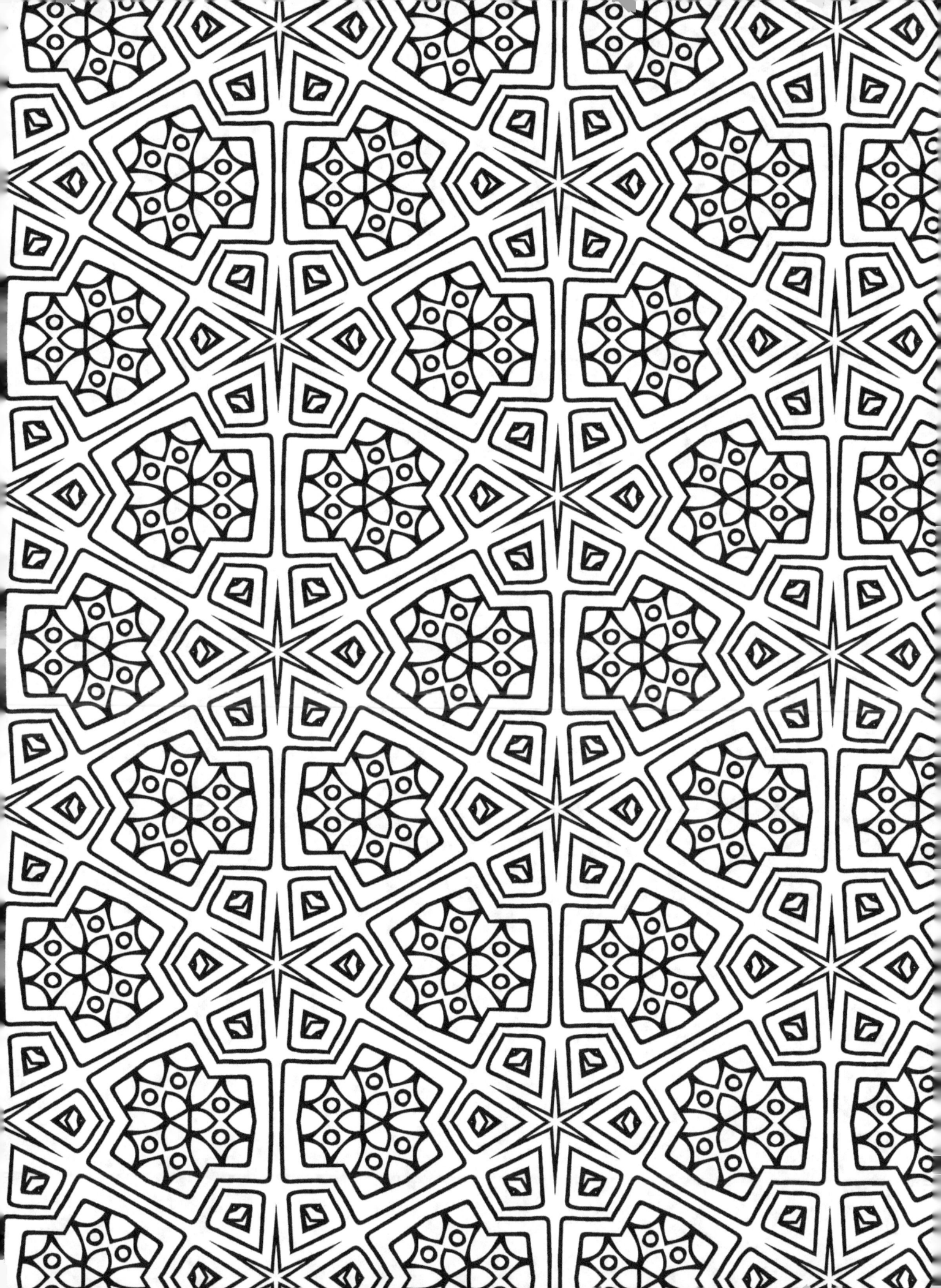

If you enjoyed colouring these designs, then move onto another book in the Progressive Patterns series of Adult Colouring Books.

We are sure you will love them!

We are amazed by the way that each of our designs looks so different when it has been coloured, so please share. We love to see your finished designs, don't be shy, head over to our Facebook page and show us what you have created.

https://www.facebook.com/progressivepatternsadultcolouringbooks

Look out for our other colouring books created by nikk nakk designs.
- Simple Styles
- Decorative Designs
- Intricate Inspirations
- Progressive Patterns Volume 1
- Progressive Patterns - A Man's World
- Fairies and Flowers

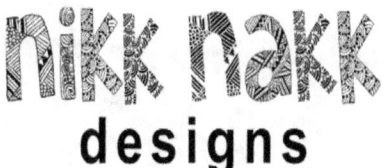